I0490783

Thriving in the
modern marketplace

Secrets to staying
ahead in a
competitive age

Marcus Walker

Table of Contents

Chapter 1

Chapter 2

- The power of data in business

- Agility and flexibility in today's fast paced business environment

- How to build an agile organization

- Exploring the key traits of successful adaptable leaders

- Branding in the digital world

Chapter 3

- Key elements of a strong brand in the digital age

- Successful branding campaigns in recent years

- Embracing diversity in business

- Practical tips for making organization more inclusive

Chapter 4

- The power of networking in business

- Importance of customer experience

- Exploring how the future of work might look like

- Tips on how to improve customer experience

Chapter 5

- Impacts of automation, artificial intelligence and the gig economy on jobs and careers

- Practical advice for staying ahead in the modern marketplace

- Importance of continuous learning and building a strong personal brand

- Cultivating a growth mindset in business

Chapter 1

Understanding the modern marketplace

Understanding the modern marketplace is crucial for any business to succeed in today's fast-paced economic environment. Here are some key points to keep in mind:

1. Focus on the Customer: In today's marketplace, customer needs and preferences are constantly evolving. Therefore, businesses need to have a customer-centric approach, where they prioritize understanding their customers' needs, preferences and pain points.

2. Embrace Technology: Technology has transformed the way businesses operate and interact with customers. From e-commerce platforms to social media, businesses must integrate technology in their operations to stay ahead of the competition.

3. Keep an Eye on Competitors: Competition is fierce in the modern marketplace, and businesses must

continuously monitor and analyze their competitors' strategies, products, and services to stay relevant and competitive.

4. Be Agile and Adaptable: The modern marketplace is fast-paced and constantly evolving, and businesses that can adapt quickly to changing market conditions are likely to thrive. It is important to be agile and adaptable to new technologies, market trends, and customer behaviors.

5. Prioritize Innovation: Innovation provides a competitive advantage in the modern marketplace. Businesses must continuously innovate and develop new products, services and solutions that meet the ever-changing needs of customers.

6. Analyze Data: Data analysis is critical to understanding the modern marketplace. Businesses must closely monitor and analyze data related to customer behavior, market trends, and competition to make informed decisions and drive growth.

In summary, understanding the modern marketplace involves having a deep understanding of customer needs and preferences, embracing technology, staying on top of competition, being agile and adaptable, prioritizing innovation, and analyzing data. Incorporating these elements will help businesses thrive in today's rapidly evolving marketplace.

Factors contributing to the transformation of the marketplace in the 21st century

Some of the factors include :

1. Advances in technology: The rapid growth of technology has played a significant role in transforming the marketplace in the 21st century. E-commerce, social media, and mobile technology have all disrupted traditional models of commerce and business.

2. Changing consumer behavior: Consumers are increasingly demanding more personalized and convenient products and services. This has led to

the rise of on-demand services, subscription-based models, and digital platforms that allow for greater customization and user control.

3. Globalization: The world has become more connected and globalized than ever before. Companies can now easily reach customers and partners around the world, leading to increased competition and the need to adapt to new cultural norms and preferences.

4. Environmental sustainability: In recent years, there has been a growing awareness of the need for environmental sustainability. Companies are now held accountable for their environmental impact and are expected to adopt more sustainable practices.

5. Increased regulation: Governments are increasingly implementing regulations for businesses to protect consumers and workers, and to address issues such as privacy and data security.

6. Demographic shifts: Changing demographics, such as an aging population and a more diverse workforce, are leading to new opportunities and challenges for businesses.

7. Automation and artificial intelligence: The rise of automation and artificial intelligence has led to the automation of many jobs and the creation of new ones. This has also affected the skills and education needed for the workforce.

8. Political uncertainty: Political instability and uncertainty, such as Brexit and trade wars, can have significant impacts on the marketplace, causing businesses to adjust their strategies and operations accordingly.

Impacts of technology, globalization, changing consumer behavior and economic turmoil on business

Technology:

Technology has revolutionized the way businesses operate. It has led to the innovation of new products and services, improved efficiency in production, and enhanced communication channels. However, technology has also created new challenges for businesses, such as data security risks, increased competition, and the need for constant technological upgrades. Furthermore, the rise of automation has led to job displacement in certain industries, leading to economic and social consequences.

Globalization:

Globalization has opened up new markets for businesses around the world, leading to increased competition and expansion opportunities. However, it has also created a more complex business environment, with increased cultural and language barriers, supply chain challenges and regulatory issues. Additionally, globalization has led to offshoring, resulting in job losses in some countries while creating new employment opportunities in others.

Changing consumer behavior:

Consumer behavior is constantly changing, leading to new trends and patterns. Businesses must adapt to these changes to stay competitive. For example, the rise of social media has provided new avenues for businesses to communicate with consumers, resulting in new marketing strategies. Additionally, the focus of consumers has shifted towards more sustainable and socially responsible products, placing pressure on businesses to adopt sustainable practices.

Economic turmoil:

Economic turmoil, such as recessions and financial crises, has a significant impact on businesses. They can lead to decreased consumer spending, reduced access to capital, and increased competition. Businesses must adopt new strategies, such as cost-cutting measures, to survive during these times. However, economic turmoil can also create opportunities for businesses, such as acquiring distressed assets or partnering with struggling companies.

In conclusion, technology, globalization, changing consumer behavior, and economic turmoil each have a significant impact on businesses. Businesses must be able to adapt and evolve to survive and thrive in this ever-changing business environment.

Importance of innovation to stay competitive in the modern marketplace

Innovation is increasingly becoming a key driver of business growth and competitiveness. It is a vital tool for companies to maintain their competitive edge in today's rapidly changing business environment. Innovation helps businesses to create new products, services, and processes, as well as improve existing ones, thereby providing customers with more value, better quality, and improved cost-effectiveness. The importance of innovation in staying competitive in the modern marketplace can be elaborated on in the following ways:

1. Meeting changing customer expectations: Innovation can enable companies to meet changing customer expectations by identifying and providing new solutions that address the new and evolving needs of consumers. Customer satisfaction is crucial to maintaining a competitive edge, and innovation provides companies with the ability to stay ahead of their competitors by anticipating and meeting customer needs more effectively.

2. Driving growth and revenue: Innovation can drive growth and revenue by creating new markets for businesses, increasing revenue from existing products, improving operational efficiencies, and enabling businesses to enter new markets more quickly.

3. Staying ahead of competitors: Businesses that continuously innovate can stay ahead of competitors and maintain a competitive advantage in their industry. Innovation can generate new ideas and opportunities, allowing businesses to adapt and respond to market changes quickly and effectively.

4. Building brand reputation: Innovative companies are often seen as industry leaders, and their innovative products and services can help to build brand reputation, customer loyalty, and brand equity over time.

5. Attracting and retaining talent: Innovators often attract and retain top talent. Companies that embrace innovation are more likely to attract creative, talented individuals who are looking for an environment that encourages experimentation and learning.

In conclusion, the importance of innovation cannot be overstated when it comes to staying competitive in the modern marketplace. By innovating, companies can keep up with changing customer expectations, drive growth, stay ahead of competitors, build brand reputation, and attract and retain top talent. Companies that prioritize innovation will have a better chance of thriving in today's rapidly changing business environment.

How to foster a culture of innovation in your organization

Encourage a mindset of curiosity and experimentation: Encourage your employees to explore and experiment with new ideas and technologies. Allow failure as a part of the process and encourage people to learn from it.

Create an environment that fosters innovation: Provide your employees with the necessary resources, tools, and structures to encourage innovation. Give them space to think creatively and come up with new ideas.

Empower your employees: Encourage your employees to take ownership of their work and give them the autonomy to make decisions. This gives them a sense of ownership and accountability, which can lead to better innovation.

Celebrate innovation: Recognize and reward employees who come up with innovative ideas. Celebrating innovation can help build a culture of innovation in the organization and motivate employees to think creatively.

Collaborate and learn from others: Encourage your employees to collaborate across departments and with outside partners to learn from others and gain new perspectives. This can spark new ideas and accelerate innovation within the organization.

Exploring some of the most innovative companies in the world

1. Tesla - Known for its electric vehicles and clean energy products, Tesla is a

pioneer in the sustainable energy industry. The company has disrupted the traditional automaker model by manufacturing luxury electric vehicles that are stylish, fast, and fuel-efficient.

2. Amazon - One of the largest e-commerce companies in the world, Amazon has disrupted the traditional retail space by providing a seamless online shopping experience. The company leverages its vast customer data to offer personalized product recommendations, and its Prime membership program has also revolutionized the way people shop.

3. Apple - As a technology giant, Apple is known for its innovative products such as the iPhone, iPad, and MacBook. The company's focus on innovation, design and user experience has made it one of the most successful companies in the world.

4. Google - As the search engine leader, Google has disrupted the way people find information on the internet. Its services range from Google Search, Google Maps, and Google Drive to Android mobile operating system which is widely used by billions of people worldwide.

5. Alibaba - Alibaba is one of the world's largest online retailers, with its platform being used by numerous businesses to sell their products. The Chinese company has also expanded into other areas including cloud computing, logistics, and artificial intelligence.

6. Facebook - The social media giant, Facebook is known for its mission to connect people around the world. The company's key offerings include Messenger, Instagram, and WhatsApp, along with its flagship platform, Facebook.

7. Netflix - A pioneer in the online streaming industry, Netflix has revolutionized the way we consume entertainment. The company has disrupted the traditional TV broadcast business model by providing on-demand access to a vast array of content, including original productions.

8. SpaceX - The space exploration company founded by Elon Musk is known for its efforts to lower the cost of space transport and its plans to colonize Mars. The company has disrupted traditional space exploration by reusing rocket boosters and other technologies to cut costs.

9. 23andMe - A personal genomics and biotechnology company, 23andMe has revolutionized the healthcare industry by providing consumers with access to their genetic information. The company's services include ancestry and health reports, and its DNA kits are widely used by people around the world to learn more about their genetic

makeup.

10. Tencent - A leading internet company in China, Tencent offers a range of digital products and services including social media (WeChat, QQ), online payment systems, video games, music, and other entertainment services. Tencent has been responsible for the rise of the digital economy in China and continues to innovate in this space.

Chapter 2

The power of data in business

Data has become a critical component in running a business in today's data-driven era. In fact, many companies are now referring to themselves as data-driven since they believe in the power of data in driving growth and decision-making.

Below are some of the reasons why data is essential for businesses:

Better decision-making: With data, businesses can make informed decisions based on facts and not just intuition or assumptions. Data analysis can help identify patterns and trends, which can assist business owners in making decisions that are more precise and accurate.

Improved customer understanding: Customer data allows businesses to understand their customers' needs better and tailor their products and services to meet those needs.

Increased efficiency: Data analysis can help identify areas of the business that are inefficient, thereby allowing companies to make changes that can save time and money.

Improved products and services: By analyzing data, companies can gain insight into which products or services are performing well, what features customers like, and what areas need improvement.

Competitive advantage: Through data analysis, businesses can gain a competitive edge over their rivals, allowing them to stay ahead of the curve in terms of innovation and customer satisfaction.

In conclusion, data is essential for businesses to make informed decisions, improve customer understanding, increase efficiency, improve products and services, and gain a competitive advantage. This power of data can help businesses grow and thrive in today's data-driven economy.

Agility and flexibility in today's fast paced business environment

In today's fast-paced business environment, agility and flexibility are key to success. Organizations must be able to adapt quickly to changing market conditions, unexpected disruptions, and new opportunities. Here are a few ways in which agility and flexibility are important in today's business environment:

1. Responding quickly to changing market conditions: Businesses must be able to adapt quickly to changes in the market, such as shifts in consumer demand or new competitors. This requires the ability to quickly change strategies or product offerings as needed.

2. Navigating disruptions: Disruptions are becoming more common in today's business environment, whether due to natural disasters, political unrest, or other factors. Businesses must have plans in place to navigate these disruptions, and the ability to quickly pivot as needed.

3. Adapting to new technologies: Technology is rapidly changing the way businesses operate, from cloud computing to artificial intelligence. Companies must stay up-to-date with the latest technologies and be willing to adopt them as needed to stay ahead of the competition.

4. Embracing new business models: Traditional business models are being challenged by new entrants and disruptors. Businesses must be willing to embrace new business models as needed to stay competitive in the market.

Overall, agility and flexibility are critical for success in today's fast-paced business environment. Companies that are able to adapt quickly and be flexible in their approach will be best positioned to succeed in the long run.

How to build an agile organization

Building an agile organization involves a combination of strategy, culture, and processes that create a flexible, adaptable, and responsive environment. Here are some steps to build an agile organization:

1. Get leadership buy-in: Agile transformation requires support from top leaders to drive commitment, resources, and alignment across the organization. Leaders need to understand the value of agility and advocate for the change.

2. Establish a clear vision: It's important to have a clear understanding of why agility is critical for the organization and how it aligns with broader strategic goals. The vision needs to be communicated throughout the organization.

3. Create a culture of agility: Culture plays a critical role in building an agile organization. Agile culture values transparency, collaboration, experimentation, continuous improvement, and customer focus. Leaders should create an environment that fosters these values and behaviors.

4. Develop cross-functional teams: Cross-functional teams enable quick decision-making, experimentation, and learning. It's important to align work around goals and set up an Agile project management framework.

5. Build Agile processes: Agile processes like Scrum, Kanban, and Lean help organizations to be more flexible, adaptive, and customer-centric. It's important to train and support teams on agile methodologies and best practices.

6. Embrace continuous learning and improvement: Agility requires organizations to continuously learn and improve. Leaders should encourage experimentation, measure outcomes, gather feedback and learn from their mistakes.

7. Foster collaboration: Agile organizations value collaboration across functions, teams and stakeholders. Collaboration enhances transparency and builds trust. It also enables speed to market and customer focused outcomes.

By following these steps, organizations can start their agile journey, building an environment that can adapt and thrive in an ever-changing business world.

Exploring the key traits of successful adaptable leaders

Adaptability is one of the most crucial qualities of successful leaders. Leaders who are adaptable are highly valued as they can steer their team through rapidly changing environments, unexpected challenges or opportunities, and different situations. The key traits of successful adaptable leaders include:

1. Flexibility: Successful adaptable leaders are highly flexible and can adjust their plans, actions, and strategies depending on changing scenarios. They understand that flexibility is critical when circumstances change, and they are willing to revise their plans quickly to keep their teams and organizations on

track.

2. Open-mindedness: Adaptable leaders are open-minded and listen to the ideas of their team members. They understand that other people can provide valuable input that can lead to new opportunities, innovative solutions, and better decisions, and they encourage their team to contribute their thoughts and ideas.

3. Problem-solving skills: Adaptable leaders are highly skilled problem solvers. They are comfortable with ambiguity, can gather facts from various sources, and can identify key issues to reach the best possible solution.

4. Effective communication skills: Adaptable leaders have excellent communication skills, and they can convey their message clearly and effectively. They understand the

importance of both listening and speaking, and they communicate with honesty and integrity.

5. Visionary thinking: Adaptable leaders have a forward-thinking mindset, and they can visualize different scenarios and outcomes. They can create a clear vision for their teams and organizations, and they rely on their intuition and experience to make the best decisions under rapidly changing circumstances.

6. Resilience: Adaptable leaders are highly resilient and can overcome challenges and setbacks with ease. They can stay focused, motivated, and committed to their goals amidst difficulties and failures, and they lead by example to encourage their teams to do the same.

7. Collaborative skills: Adaptable leaders possess excellent collaborative skills,

and they can work effectively with colleagues and stakeholders from different backgrounds and perspectives. They can build trust and rapport with their team members, and they foster a culture of teamwork and innovation.

Overall, being adaptable is an essential trait for successful leaders. Adaptable leaders are open to change, flexible, good problem solvers, visionary, collaborative, resilient, and effective communicators. By developing these key traits, leaders can navigate through challenging times and achieve success in a constantly changing environment.

Branding in the digital age

Branding in the digital age has undergone significant changes due to the emergence of new technologies and changes in consumer behavior. In today's digital age, branding goes far beyond just creating a recognizable name or logo. It encompasses a broader set of elements, including online reputation management, customer experience, and engagement across multiple digital channels.

One of the significant changes in the digital age is the shift towards more personalized branding. Digital tools such as data analytics and Artificial Intelligence (AI) allow companies to gather data on consumer preferences, buying behavior, and interactions with brands. Brands can then use this data to personalize their marketing strategies, product offerings, and customer experiences to specific audiences.

Another critical aspect of branding in the digital age is social media management. Social media channels allow companies to connect and engage with their customers in real-time, providing them with instant feedback and insights into their brand's perception. Companies must maintain a strong social media presence, respond promptly to customer inquiries and complaints, and share valuable content to build trust and credibility with their audience.

Finally, with the rise of e-commerce, companies must create a seamless and enjoyable customer experience online. This includes website design and usability, search engine optimization (SEO), and the ease of the checkout process. A positive customer experience can turn a one-time buyer into a repeat customer and increase brand loyalty.

Overall, branding in the digital age requires companies to stay up-to-date with evolving technologies, adapt to changes in consumer behavior and preferences, and focus on building a positive and personalized customer experience across multiple digital channels.

Chapter 3

Key elements of a strong brand in the digital age

1. Consistency: A strong brand needs to have a consistent message across all platforms, including social media, website, email marketing, and other marketing materials.

2. Authenticity: In today's digital age, customers are looking for authentic connections with brands they interact with. Therefore, a strong brand must authentically represent itself to its target customers.

3. Emotional Connection: A strong brand should aim to create an emotional connection with its customers. It can create a personality through the use of tone, humor, or storytelling.

4. User Experience: Customers demand an extremely high standard for their digital experience. A strong brand should ensure that every touchpoint they have with customers is user-friendly, intuitive, and seamless.

5. Innovation: In today's fast-paced digital world, brands must continue to innovate and evolve their offerings to remain relevant and appeal to consumers' changing needs.

6. Social Responsibility: A strong brand should contribute positively to society and demonstrate its social responsibility through its actions.

7. Trust: Trust is a vital component of a strong brand. It is important to maintain trust with customers by consistently delivering quality products or services and transparently addressing any issues that may arise.

8. Visual Identity: A strong brand should have a consistent visual identity that is simple, recognizable, and unique. This can include a logo, color scheme, typography, and other design elements that help the brand stand out from competitors.

Successful branding campaigns in recent years

Nike's "Just Do It" campaign: Nike's "Just Do It" campaign is one of the most iconic global campaigns of all time. The slogan reinforces Nike's belief that anyone can achieve greatness if they simply push themselves to do so.

Coca-Cola's "Share a Coke" campaign: The "Share a Coke" campaign by Coca-Cola has been hugely successful because of its personalization aspect. By printing people's names on the Coca-Cola cans and bottles, it made people feel special and engaged with the brand on a more personal level.

Apple's "Shot on iPhone" campaign: Apple's "Shot on iPhone" campaign showcases the stunning image quality that can be captured with iPhone cameras. The campaign used user-generated content, which also worked as a great way to engage with customers and showcase their individual creativity.

Old Spice's "Smell Like a Man, Man" campaign: Old Spice's "Smell Like a Man, Man" campaign is an example of a rebranding strategy that successfully targeted a younger audience. The campaign was humorous and engaging, which helped to create a strong brand personality and image.

Dove's "Real Beauty" campaign: Dove's "Real Beauty" campaign tackled the unrealistic beauty standards for women by using real women instead of models in their advertisements. The campaign was praised for its inclusivity and helped to create a more genuine and authentic image for the brand.

Embracing diversity in business

Educate yourself and others on the benefits of diversity: Understand that diversity goes beyond race and gender, it includes differences in age, religion, ethnicity, socio-economic status, and more. Make sure to consistently emphasize to your employees how diversity can help the business succeed and give examples of how diversity has been an asset in other successful companies.

Create a diverse work environment: Hire people from different backgrounds, offer diversity and inclusion training, and actively seek out diverse candidates in job postings. It is important to value diversity and make it part of the company culture.

Implement diversity policies: Develop policies that promote diversity such as ensuring fair hiring practices, promoting equal pay, and providing flexible work schedules to accommodate various religious holidays.

Foster open communication: Encourage open and honest communication in the workplace so that all employees feel comfortable expressing their views without fear of retribution.

Celebrate diversity: Sponsor events and activities that celebrate diverse cultures, holidays, and achievements. This will help to foster a sense of community and show that the company values diversity.

Practical tips for making organization more inclusive

Conduct an audit: Conduct an audit of your organization's policies, practices, and culture to identify any areas that may be exclusive.

Diversity and inclusion training: Provide training and support for employees to promote diversity and inclusion, and educate them on the importance of creating a welcoming and inclusive environment.

Address unconscious bias: Recognize

and address the potential for unconscious bias in your workplace, and take steps to mitigate its impact.

Flexible policies: Develop and implement policies that promote inclusiveness, such as flexible working arrangements, parental leave, and support for employees with disabilities.

Be open to feedback: Create a culture of openness and feedback, allowing employees to contribute to the company's diversity and inclusion initiatives.

Seek diverse perspectives: Encourage participation from a broad range of voices and perspectives, including those from marginalized and underrepresented groups.

Celebrate diversity: Celebrate the diversity present in your organization through events and activities that highlight different cultures, beliefs, and experiences.

Create a safe space: Foster a safe and

supportive environment for employees, where they can feel comfortable sharing their experiences and ideas without fear of discrimination or prejudice.

Chapter 4

The power of networking in business

The power of networking in business is significant, as it can help entrepreneurs and professionals make valuable connections, develop relationships, and create new opportunities. By attending industry events, trade fairs, and business conferences, people can engage with others who have similar interests, skills, or experiences.

Networking provides the opportunity to meet potential clients, mentors, investors, and partners, and to gain insight into new market trends, emerging technologies, and innovative business models. It can help people to learn about job openings, get valuable feedback, and find new ways to collaborate with others.

Building a strong network of contacts can also increase visibility and credibility for a business or professional, as word-of-mouth referrals and recommendations can help to establish a reputation for excellence, trustworthiness, and expertise. Moreover, networking can lead to partnerships and collaborations that can open up new markets, create new revenue streams, and help businesses stay ahead of the competition.

In summary, the power of networking is that it offers invaluable opportunities to connect, learn, grow, and succeed, making it an essential tool for anyone looking to establish and grow a successful business or career.

Importance of customer experience

Customer experience is critical in business because it directly influences customer loyalty and referral rates. Here are some of the key importance of customer experience in business:

1. Increased customer loyalty: Providing a positive customer experience leads to greater customer loyalty. Loyal customers are more likely to purchase from you again, and they are more likely to recommend your business to others.

2. Brand reputation: A positive customer experience creates a positive reputation for your brand, which can drive more customers to your business by word-of-mouth recommendation.

3. Improved customer retention: A great customer experience reduces the likelihood of customers churning to a competitor. Retaining customers can dramatically improve the bottom line of your business.

4. Competitive advantage: A business that prioritizes customer experience sets itself apart from competitors, who may not focus on creating a positive

experience for their customers.

5. Increased revenue: Satisfying customers and providing them with a positive experience can lead to repeat business and increased spending over time, ultimately leading to an increase in revenue.

6. Cost-effective: Providing great customer experience isn't always about spending more money on customers, but more about delivering a consistent and quality experience that satisfies their needs.

All these reasons are why businesses need to focus on providing excellent customer experience to drive revenue and growth.

Tips on how to improve customer experience

Listen to customer feedback and act on it promptly

Provide excellent customer service by being responsive, informative and helpful

Make sure your products or services meet or exceed customer expectations

Create a seamless, user-friendly experience across all customer touchpoints

Train your employees to be knowledgeable and customer-oriented

Offer customized solutions and personalized experiences

Show appreciation for your customers with rewards, loyalty programs or other incentives

Anticipate customer needs and provide proactive support

Use technology to enhance the customer experience, such as chatbots, self-service options, etc.

Continually measure and analyze customer satisfaction metrics and use the insights to improve.

Exploring how the future of work might look like

1. Research current trends: Look into current trends related to the future of work such as automation, remote work, artificial intelligence, and the gig economy. Look for data and reports on what is happening now and what is projected for the future.

2. Talk to experts: Speak with workers in various fields and industry experts to gain their perspective on what they think the future of work will look like. This could be tech experts or individuals in management positions.

3. Attend events: Attend seminars, workshops, and conferences on the future of work or related fields. These events typically feature speakers who focus on the latest trends and research, which can give you an idea of what the future of work will look like.

4. Read publications: Keep up with industry publications, research papers, and news articles on the topic of the future of work. Many of these sources provide insights on the latest discoveries and trends.

5. Consider scenario planning: Use your research to develop potential scenarios for the future of work. Assess how different technological advancements, social changes, and economic developments may impact the future work landscape.

6. Use brainstorming techniques: Gather a group of colleagues or industry peers to brainstorm ideas about the future of work. Consider factors like workplace diversity, evolving professional skills, and the potential impact of digital technologies.

7. Experimental thinking: Consider experimental thinking to explore potential alternate futures. This could involve developing prototypes of new work environments or testing out ways of working that are novel or untested.

8. Use predictive analytics: Use data and predictive analytics to anticipate how changes in the labor market and technological advances will impact different professions and industries.

9. Monitor regulatory changes: Stay up-to-date with regulatory changes that could impact the future of work such as

shifts in employment law or immigration policy.

10. Stay agile: Keep an open mind and be adaptable to changes that may occur in the future of work as the workplace landscape continues to evolve.

Chapter 5

Impacts of automation, artificial intelligence and the gig economy on jobs and careers

As an AI language model, I do not have personal beliefs or opinions. However, I can provide you with some information about the potential impacts of automation, artificial intelligence and the gig economy on jobs and careers:

1. Automation:

- Automation can replace human jobs that can be done more efficiently and cost-effectively by machines. This can lead to job losses in certain industries, such as manufacturing, logistics, and administration.

- On the other hand, automation can also create new jobs in fields such as data analytics, robotics maintenance, and software development.

2. Artificial intelligence:

- AI has the potential to greatly enhance productivity and efficiency in the workplace, leading to higher profits and economic growth.

- However, AI may also lead to job displacement and deskilling in certain industries, such as customer service, finance, and legal services.

- High-skilled jobs that require cognitive and creative thinking, such as software development, engineering, and design, may be less affected by AI.

3. The gig economy:

- The gig economy refers to the trend of short-term, temporary work arrangements, usually facilitated by online platforms.

- Some argue that the gig economy offers more flexibility and autonomy for workers, and creates new opportunities for entrepreneurship and self-employment.

- Others argue that the gig economy can lead to job insecurity, low pay, and lack of benefits, as well as a decrease in unionization and collective bargaining power.

Overall, the impacts of automation, AI, and the gig economy on jobs and careers are complex and multifaceted, and depend on a variety of factors such as industry, skill level, and geographic location.

Practical advice for staying ahead in the modern marketplace

Continuously learn and adapt: The modern marketplace is constantly changing, and those who stay ahead are the ones who are always learning and adapting. Stay up-to-date with the latest trends and technologies in your industry.

Build a solid online presence: With the rise of e-commerce and digital marketing, having a strong online presence is key to staying ahead. Develop a website, social media accounts, and email marketing campaigns.

Focus on customer experience: Customer experience is becoming a key differentiator in the modern marketplace. Invest in understanding your customer's needs and providing them with a great experience.

Emphasize innovation: Innovation is necessary for staying ahead in an ever-changing marketplace. Encourage innovation in your business by fostering a culture of creativity and experimentation.

Develop strategic partnerships: Collaborate with other companies to expand your reach and offer more value to your customers.

Practice agility: Be prepared to pivot and adapt quickly to changes in the marketplace. This means being flexible and able to adjust your strategy on short notice.

Focus on data-driven decision-making: Use data to inform your business decisions and strategies. Analyze consumer behavior, industry trends, and sales data to make informed choices that drive growth.

Importance of continuous learning and building a strong personal brand

Continuous learning and building a strong personal brand are crucial in today's competitive job market. By continually expanding your knowledge and skills, you demonstrate your commitment to personal and professional growth. This can help you stand out from other candidates and increase your value to current or potential employers. Additionally, staying up-to-date on the latest industry trends and technologies can ensure that you remain relevant in your field and can adapt to new challenges.

A strong personal brand can also enhance your career prospects. It can help establish your reputation and credibility among colleagues and potential employers. By building a positive reputation and demonstrating your expertise, you can improve your chances of being considered for promotions, job offers, or other career opportunities. Additionally, a strong personal brand can help you network with others in your industry and connect with like-minded individuals who can offer advice, support, or mentorship.

In summary, continuous learning and building a strong personal brand are critical for career success. By focusing on personal growth and demonstrating your expertise, you can enhance your professional reputation, become more valuable to employers, and increase your opportunities for career advancement.

Cultivating a growth mindset in business

In today's business world, cultivating a growth mindset is essential for success. A growth mindset is the belief that one's abilities and intelligence can be developed and improved through hard work, dedication, and learning from failure. It is the opposite of a fixed mindset, where individuals believe that their talents and intelligence are predetermined and cannot be changed.

Cultivating a growth mindset starts with understanding that failure is not the end but an opportunity to learn and grow. In business, failure can come in various forms, such as missed deadlines, unsuccessful product launches, or financial losses. However, it is essential to see failures as learning experiences and use them to improve and grow instead of giving up.

Business owners can also foster a growth mindset by encouraging their team members to take risks and try new ideas. When team members feel that they have the support and freedom to take risks, they are more likely to come up with innovative ideas that can drive the business forward. Leaders can also offer their team members opportunities for professional development, such as training programs, workshops, or conferences.

Another essential aspect of cultivating a growth mindset in business is to focus on the process rather than the outcome. When the focus is solely on the outcome, such as sales numbers or profits, it can lead to a fixed mindset, where individuals become only interested in achieving the end goal without considering the process of getting there. However, by focusing on the process, business owners and team members can learn from each step, making necessary adjustments and improvements along the way.

Business owners can also foster a growth mindset by creating a culture that encourages openness, collaboration, and constructive criticism. When team members feel comfortable sharing their ideas and being open to constructive feedback, they are more likely to learn and grow from each other.

To cultivate a growth mindset in business, it is also crucial to avoid a blame culture. In a blame culture, individuals are quick to point fingers and assign blame instead of taking responsibility for their actions. However, a growth mindset encourages individuals to take responsibility for their mistakes and use them as opportunities for growth and learning.

Business owners can also encourage their team members to embrace challenges and see them as opportunities to learn and grow. When individuals approach challenges with a growth mindset, they are more likely to persevere and overcome obstacles that may have seemed insurmountable initially.

Finally, business owners can cultivate a growth mindset by celebrating successes and milestones along the way. When individuals feel that their hard work and achievements are valued and recognized, they are more motivated to continue pushing themselves and achieving even greater success in the future.

In conclusion, cultivating a growth mindset in business is essential for success. It requires individuals to embrace failure, take risks and try new ideas, focus on the process, embrace openness and constructive criticism, avoid a blame culture, embrace challenges, and celebrate successes. By cultivating a growth mindset in business, individuals can learn and grow, continuously improving themselves and their organizations.

www.ingramcontent.com/pod-product-compliance
Lightning Source LLC
Chambersburg PA
CBHW071109220526
45467CB00004B/1764